Website

Username

Password

Notes

Website

Username

Password

Notes

Website

Username

Password

Notes

A

Website

Username

Password

Notes

Website

Username

Password

Notes

Website

Username

Password

Notes

Website

Username

Password

Notes

Website

Username

Password

Notes

"May the flowers remind us why the rain is necessary."

Anonymous

A

Website

Username

Password

Notes

Website

Username

Password

Notes

Website

Username

Password

Notes

Website

Username

Password

Notes

Website

Username

Password

Notes

Website

Username

Password

Notes

"Make time for the things you love, and do things that make your soul happy!"

Jera Brandvig

---•---

Website

Username

Password

Notes

---•---

Website

Username

Password

Notes

Website

Username

Password

Notes

Website

Username

Password

Notes

Website

Username

Password

Notes

B

Website

Username

Password

Notes

_____

Website

Username

Password

Notes

_____

Website

Username

Password

Notes

C

Website

Username

Password

Notes

Website

Username

Password

Notes

Website

Username

Password

Notes

Website

Username

Password

Notes

Website

Username

Password

Notes

Website

Username

Password

Notes

Website

Username

Password

Notes

Website

Username

Password

Notes

Website

Username

Password

Notes

C

Website

Username

Password

Notes

Website

Username

Password

Notes

Website

Username

Password

Notes

Website

Username

Password

Notes

Website

Username

Password

Notes

Website

Username

Password

Notes

Website

Username

Password

Notes

---

*"Fill your heart
with what's important and
forget about the rest!"*

Jera Brandvig

Website

Username

Password

Notes

Website

Username

Password

Notes

Website

Username

Password

Notes

Website

Username

Password

Notes

D

Website

Username

Password

Notes

———————○———————

Website

Username

Password

Notes

———————○———————

Website

Username

Password

Notes

Website

Username

Password

Notes

Website

Username

Password

Notes

Website

Username

Password

Notes

E

Website

Username

Password

Notes

———○———

Website

Username

Password

Notes

———○———

Website

Username

Password

Notes

Website

Username

Password

Notes

E

————o————

Website

Username

Password

Notes

————o————

Website

Username

Password

Notes

E

Website

Username

Password

Notes

———o———

Website

Username

Password

Notes

———o———

Website

Username

Password

Notes

Website

Username

Password

Notes

Website

Username

Password

Notes

Website

Username

Password

Notes

F

Website

Username

Password

Notes

Website

Username

Password

Notes

Website

Username

Password

Notes

"It's not about having time. It's about making time. If it is important, you will find a way."

Jera Brandvig

———◦———

Website

Username

Password

Notes

———◦———

Website

Username

Password

Notes

F

Website

Username

Password

Notes

Website

Username

Password

Notes

Website

Username

Password

Notes

Website

Username

Password

Notes

G

Website

Username

Password

Notes

Website

Username

Password

Notes

Website

Username

Password

Notes

G

Website

Username

Password

Notes

Website

Username

Password

Notes

Website

Username

Password

Notes

Website

Username

Password

Notes

Website

Username

Password

Notes

Website

Username

Password

Notes

G

Website

Username

Password

Notes

Website

Username

Password

Notes

Website

Username

Password

Notes

Website

Username

Password

Notes

Website

Username

Password

Notes

> *"Keep it simple.*
> *Keep it honest. Keep it real."*
>
> Anonymous

H

———○———

Website

Username

Password

Notes

———○———

Website

Username

Password

Notes

Website

Username

Password

Notes

———○———

Website

Username

Password

Notes

———○———

Website

Username

Password

Notes

H

Website

Username

Password

Notes

Website

Username

Password

Notes

Website

Username

Password

Notes

Website

Username

Password

Notes

Website

Username

Password

Notes

Website

Username

Password

Notes

Website

Username

Password

Notes

I

Website

Username

Password

Notes

Website

Username

Password

Notes

Website

Username

Password

Notes

Website

Username

Password

Notes

Website

Username

Password

Notes

Website

Username

Password

Notes

J

Website

Username

Password

Notes

Website

Username

Password

Notes

Website

Username

Password

Notes

———○———

Website

Username

Password

Notes

———○———

Website

Username

Password

Notes

Website

Username

Password

Notes

Website

Username

Password

Notes

Website

Username

Password

Notes

Website

Username

Password

Notes

———o———

*"On a bad day
there's always lipstick."*

Audrey Hepburn

———o———

Website

Username

Password

Notes

K

Website

Username

Password

Notes

———○———

Website

Username

Password

Notes

———○———

Website

Username

Password

Notes

Website

Username

Password

Notes

Website

Username

Password

Notes

L

Website

Username

Password

Notes

Website

Username

Password

Notes

Website

Username

Password

Notes

Website

Username

Password

Notes

Website

Username

Password

Notes

———○———

Website

Username

Password

Notes

L

———○———

Website

Username

Password

Notes

Website

Username

Password

Notes

Website

L

Username

Password

Notes

Website

Username

Password

Notes

Website

Username

Password

Notes

Website

Username

Password

M

Notes

Website

Username

Password

Notes

Website

Username

Password

Notes

———·———

Website

Username

M

Password

Notes

———·———

Website

Username

Password

Notes

Website

Username

Password

Notes

Website

Username

Password

Notes

M

Website

Username

Password

Notes

Website

Username

Password

Notes

Website

Username

M

Password

Notes

Website

Username

Password

Notes

Website

Username

Password

Notes

⎯⎯⎯ ○ ⎯⎯⎯

Website

Username

Password

Notes

⎯⎯⎯ ○ ⎯⎯⎯

Website

Username

Password

Notes

Website _____

Username _____

Password _____

Notes _____

_____

_____

_____

———o———

Website _____

Username _____

Password _____

Notes _____

_____

_____

_____

N

———o———

"You are always responsible for how you act, no matter how you feel. Remember that."

Anonymous

Website

Username

Password

Notes

Website

Username

Password

Notes

Website

Username

Password

Notes

Website

Username

Password

Notes

———————o———————

Website

Username

Password

Notes

N

———————o———————

Website

Username

Password

Notes

Website

Username

Password

Notes

Website

Username

Password

Notes

O

Website

Username

Password

Notes

Website

Username

Password

Notes

Website

Username

Password

Notes

O

Website

Username

Password

Notes

Website

Username

Password

Notes

Website

Username

Password

Notes

Website

Username

Password

Notes

Website

Username

Password

Notes

―――――○―――――

Website

Username

Password

Notes

P

―――――○―――――

Website

Username

Password

Notes

> *"Don't be afraid to
> 'quilt' outside the box!"*

Jera Brandvig

———o———

Website

Username

Password

Notes

Q

———o———

Website

Username

Password

Notes

Website

Username

Password

Notes

Website

Username

Password

Notes

Q

Website

Username

Password

Notes

Website

Username

Password

Notes

Website

Username

Password

Notes

R

Website

Username

Password

Notes

Website

Username

Password

Notes

Website

Username

Password

Notes

R

Website

Username

Password

Notes

Website

Username

Password

Notes

Website

Username

Password

Notes

S

Website

Username

Password

Notes

Website

Username

Password

Notes

Website

Username

Password

Notes

S

Website

Username

Password

Notes

Website

Username

Password

Notes

Website

Username

Password

Notes

Website

Username

Password

Notes

S

Website

Username

Password

Notes

———————— o ————————

Website

Username

Password

Notes

———————— o ————————

S

Website

Username

Password

Notes

Website

Username

Password

Notes

Website

Username

Password

Notes

"Where land and sea meet is this city. Ferries come and go. The Cascades misty glow. The smell of the sea, and freshly brewing coffee. Are all reflected on this city."

Jera Brandvig

(from *The Emerald City* Quilt in *Quilt As-you-Go Made Modern*)

Website

Username

Password

Notes

———————o———————

Website

Username

Password

Notes

———————o———————

Website

Username

Password

Notes

Website

Username

Password

Notes

Website

Username

Password

Notes

Website

Username

Password

Notes

Website

Username

Password

Notes

Website

Username

Password

Notes

Website

Username

Password

Notes

Website

Username

Password

Notes

Website

Username

Password

Notes

Website

Username

Password

Notes

U

Website

Username

Password

Notes

---◦---

"Learn the rules like a pro so you can break them like an artist."

Anonymous

---◦---

Website

Username

Password

Notes

Website

Username

Password

Notes

Website

Username

Password

Notes

Website

Username

Password

Notes

V

Website

Username

Password

Notes

Website

Username

Password

Notes

Website

Username

Password

Notes

V

Website

Username

Password

Notes

Website

Username

Password

Notes

Website

Username

Password

Notes

W

Website

Username

Password

Notes

Website

Username

Password

Notes

Website

Username

Password

Notes

W

Website

Username

Password

Notes

Website

Username

Password

Notes

Website

Username

Password

Notes

Website _____

Username _____

Password _____

Notes _____

_____

_____

_____

———————o———————

Website _____

Username _____

Password _____

Notes _____

_____

_____

_____

———————o———————

Website _____

Username _____

Password _____

Notes _____

_____

_____

_____

"Break free from following the 'rules' and embrace your inner creativity to make a one-of-a-kind quilt!"

Jera Brandvig

———————○———————

Website

Username

Password

Notes

———————○———————

Website

Username

Password

Notes

Website

Username

Password

Notes

———○———

Website

Username

Password

Notes

———○———

Website

Username

Password

Notes

Website

Username

Password

Notes

Website

Username

Password

Notes

Website

Username

Password

Notes

Website

Username

Password

Notes

Website

Username

Password

Notes

Website

Username

Password

Notes